Eating Apples

by

Gail Saunders-Smith

Pebble Books

an imprint of Capstone Press

Pebble Books

Pebble Books are published by Capstone Press
818 North Willow Street, Mankato, Minnesota 56001
http://www.capstone-press.com
Copyright © 1998 by Capstone Press
All Rights Reserved • Printed in the United States of America

Library of Congress Cataloging-in-Publication Data
Saunders-Smith, Gail.
   Eating apples/by Gail Saunders-Smith.
      p. cm.
   Includes bibliographical references and index.
   Summary: Simple text and photographs describe different
ways to enjoy apples--whole, sliced, cooked, and juiced.
   ISBN 1-56065-582-8
   1. Cookery (Apples)--Juvenile literature. [1. Apples.
2. Cookery--Apples.] I. Title.

TX813.A6S28 1998
641.6'411--dc21   97-29799
                                        CIP
                                        AC

Editorial Credits

Lois Wallentine, editor; Timothy Halldin and James Franklin,
design; Michelle L. Norstad, photo research

Photo Credits

Michelle Coughlan, 1, 4, 8, 12, 14
Unicorn Stock/Jean Higgins, cover; Paul A. Hein, 6; Doris
   Brookes, 10; David Cummings, 16; Pamela Pruett-Power, 18;
   Chuck Schmeiser, 20

Table of Contents

Raw Apples. 5

Cooked Apples. 9

Liquid Apples. 15

Fun Apples 19

Words to Know 22

Read More 23

Internet Sites. 23

Note to Parents and Teachers . . 24

Index/Word List. 24

apples

6

apple slices

8

apple pie

apple crisp

apple sauce

apple juice

apple cider

caramel apple

apple fun

Words to Know

caramel—a candy made from burnt sugar, butter, and milk; caramel is sometimes used to coat whole apples.

cider—a drink made from pressed apples

crisp—a dessert made from fruit and a crumbled crust

juice—a drink made from the liquid of fruit or vegetables

pie—a dessert made from fruit and a pastry crust

sauce—fruit that is cooked until soft

Read More

Burckhardt, Ann L. *Apples.* Mankato, Minn.: Bridgestone Books, 1996.

Gibbons, Gail. *The Seasons of Arnold's Apple Tree.* San Diego: Harcourt Brace Jovanovich, 1984.

Micucci, Charles. *The Life and Times of the Apple.* New York: Orchard Books, 1992.

Internet Sites

Apples: A Guide to Selection and Use
http://www.ag.ohio-state.edu/~ohioline/
hyg-fact/1000/1402.html

Apple Recipes
http://www.seanet.com/Users/tberry/recipe.html

Dictionary: Apple
http://www.epicurious.com/db/dictionary/terms/a/
apple.html

Note to Parents and Teachers

This book illustrates and describes types of food made from apples. The text is clearly depicted in the photographs. The clear photographs support the beginning reader in making and maintaining the meaning of the simple text. Children may need assistance in using the Table of Contents, Words to Know, Read More, Internet Sites, and Index/Word List sections of the book.

Index/Word List

apple, 5, 7, 9, 11, 13, 15, 17, 19, 21
caramel, 19
cider, 17
crisp, 11
fun, 21
juice, 15
pie, 9
sauce, 13
slices, 7

Word Count: 17
Early-Intervention Level: 3